STORYLINE
IRELAND

BOOK 4

Felicity Hayes-McCoy
John McArdle
Sam McBratney
Gerard Woulfe

Oliver & Boyd

Acknowledgements

The publishers gratefully acknowledge the special help and advice of the following in preparing this series for publication: Bernagh Brims, BBC Schools Radio, Northern Ireland; Richard Byrne, St Mary's (Boys) School, Navan; and Ursula Daly, Educational Company of Ireland.

We are grateful to the following for supplying photographs and information and giving permission for their use: Bord Failte/Irish Tourist Board, p82; The National Gallery of Ireland, p73; Trinity College, Dublin, p32.

Illustrated by Bob Geary, Trevor Ridley, Willie Rodgers, Gwen Tourret, Graham Townsend, Barry Wilkinson.

Oliver & Boyd
Robert Stevenson House
1-3 Baxter's Place
Leith Walk
Edinburgh EH1 3BB

A Division of Longman Group UK Ltd.

ISBN 0 05 004046 4

First Published 1988

Set in 12/18 Monophoto Plantin 110
Produced by Longman Group (F.E.) Ltd
Printed in Hong Kong

He was a sallow little fellow, his skin the colour of old mushrooms. His eyes were quick and brown under thick bushes of flaming red eyebrow. Untidy bunches of the same fiery red hair bristled out beneath the brim of his hat.

Plain-looking he certainly was, but he was most colourfully dressed: wide-brimmed black hat, plum-coloured frock coat, moss-green knee breeches, and mustard-yellow stockings.

"You're not! You can't be! There's no such thing!" Festy gasped in astonishment.

The little man spoke in a hard voice, like two pebbles striking against each other:

"What am I not?"

"A leprechaun," Festy giggled.

"I am Kinkeen Roe, coach to the hurling team of the fairies of Connacht," said the little man proudly.

"Oh, is that so?" Festy asked, and it was plain that he didn't believe it.

The little man raised a twisted ram's horn to his lips and played a sweet melody. Festy was soon lost in the turns and runs of the magic tune and all doubt left his mind. He became helpless under the spell of the fairy music.

"Follow me," Kinkeen ordered when the music had thrown its spell. He turned on his heel and scampered up the field at a brisk pace. Festy climbed over the fence and followed. He had no trouble in keeping up with the fairy, his stride being so much longer than the little man's.

Through fields they went, over stone walls, past

houses, by the banks of rivers, always westward until they came to a great flat bog that stretched for miles on every side. Kinkeen Roe ran lightly across the spongy ground and Festy followed.

As they drew near the centre of the great plain, Festy saw what looked like a clump of bog cotton stirring in the breeze. It proved, however, to be a great crowd of fairy people. Some of them had hurleys and it was clear that a match was about to begin.

"Here we are at last," said Kinkeen Roe. "The Munster fairies and the Connacht fairies are playing the great hurling match tonight. It cannot take place without a human player on each side. You, Festy McDyer, will stand in goal for Connacht, and a foxy man from Cork will man the gap for Munster."

He led Festy to the north end of the plain and there ordered him to stand between two thorn trees about a hundred yards apart.

"There's your goal now," he said, "and guard it for all you are worth."

The match began at the centre of the plain, about two miles from Festy's goal. At that distance the players looked like a clutter of leaves whirling in wind.

They came close to Festy's goal, and suddenly there was a mighty roar. The Munster fairies were throwing their hurleys in the air with delight. The ball had whizzed inside Festy's right-hand goal marker for the first score of the game.

Kinkeen was beside him at once.

"Now there, wake up," he said in his stone-chat voice. "If you let the ball through as easily as that, your team mates will be angry. Don't know what they'll do.

"To the game now! Keep your eye on the play. Move to the side of the goal nearest to the play, it doesn't matter how far away it is.

"That's right. Now to the left a little. There – yes – there. Now you have it."

The play was again coming towards them, the group of players chasing the ball from side to side of the plain.

"Now," Kinkeen prompted, "watch the player who is about to strike the ball. Watch how he places his feet. Near foot forward, ball flies across his body; back foot forward, ball flies away from his body. Watch his back-swing: high back-swing, low ball; low back-swing, high ball."

The struggling players were again quite near when the ball flashed out to a Munster fairy, bald and red-faced. He turned, near foot forward, and Festy dashed across the goal to intercept the ball. The bald fairy raised his hurley high on the back-swing.

"Low," Festy muttered to himself and crouched.

Sure enough, the ball came about knee high to where Festy was standing and he stopped it with ease.

Afterwards the play swung from goal to goal. Festy, acting on Kinkeen's instructions managed to keep the ball out at his end. The Corkman at the other end was not so lucky. Two goals were scored against him.

As the sky paled before the dawn, the Connacht fairies looked towards their human goalkeeper and, raising their hurleys above their heads, cheered in triumph. The Munster fairies hung their heads and rushed like a flowing stream through a gap in the hills to the south.

When Festy looked around again, he was alone. The Connacht fairies had vanished too.

At midday he arrived home wondering whether it had all been a dream.

Festy played very well as goalkeeper for his village hurling team that summer. He was selected for the Galway county team, and by the time they reached the All-Ireland final against Kilkenny his name was known in every corner of the land.

On All-Ireland final day the Galway team in their maroon shirts ran on to the green sod of Croke Park.

Festy McDyer, their goalkeeper, in white with maroon collar and cuffs was last man out of the tunnel. He was as proud as a peacock.

The excitement was almost unbearable for the players. A continuous roar came from seventy thousand throats, and flags waved all round the packed terraces and stands.

Festy stood on his goal line, repeating to himself the advice he had got from Kinkeen Roe in the bog of Shannawona months before. He did this before all matches.

It was near the end of the first half. Festy had played well. Twice he saved from a thin Kilkenny man with a black moustache.

Then a ball came in high from centre-field. It seemed to hang forever in the air. The goalmouth was crowded when the ball came down, and, in the struggle to win it, all the players fell to the ground. Festy was at the bottom of the heap. His head struck the ground and he was dazed for a moment.

When he came to, he was aware of a mighty cheering on the stands and terraces. The players were running out from goal, the black-and-amber-shirted ones jumping with delight. It was then that he looked around and saw the white ball nestling in the net. A goal for Kilkenny!

Festy hit the ball down field, but almost immediately it was returned. The Kilkenny man with the black moustache got it, eluded two maroon-shirted players and struck it towards goal. Festy was out of position and the ball was again in the net.

He was bewildered. He did not know what he should do to keep the ball out. It was as if he had never learned how to keep goal.

Then above all the din he heard a voice like two pebbles striking together.

"Back where we started," the voice said. It came from above his head.

He looked up. There was Kinkeen Roe standing on the crossbar and leaning against the left upright. The young man was as surprised as when he first saw him.

"Who are you?" he asked in astonishment.

"Come on, boy. Wake up. Shake your head. Let your mind go back, back, back, back to the bog of Shannawona."

Festy could faintly recall the night of the fairy match, but the details were not clear.

"Help me," he pleaded. "I have forgotten everything. My team will be terribly disappointed if I fail them."

"Now here they come," the fairy warned. "Eye on the ball. Move with the play," and he repeated the instructions he gave that night on the bog.

The Kilkenny man with the black moustache got the ball and shot for goal. It came fast and sped towards the left corner, but Festy was there. He caught it in his hand, and with a graceful, wristy stroke sent it down field. The referee whistled for half time.

When they came out for the second half, Festy ran to the goal at the other end of the field. He had fully recovered from the effects of the fall, and repeated the fairy's advice under his breath.

Kinkeen Roe had changed ends too. He was sitting on the cross bar, his legs dangling.

"I'm all right now," Festy told him. "You can go away. The people will go wild if you stay there."

"Don't worry about the people. No one but you can see me. I'll not go away until the match is over. The Connacht fairies sent me, and I daren't go back if you lose the match for Galway."

As the end of the game approached, Galway led by two points. Kilkenny needed a goal to win. They came looking for it. By clever play they managed to give the ball to their star forward, the man with the black moustache. He struck swiftly at close range, before Festy could guess the flight-path of the ball. It passed the goalkeeper's outstretched hurley travelling as fast as

a bullet from a gun.

His heart missed a beat. But then he heard a wild yell of pain. The ball struck Kinkeen Roe's instep and dropped down into Festy's hand. He hit it down field, then turned to comfort Kinkeen who had been knocked from his perch on the crossbar. At that moment the fairy was hopping on one leg around the goal area screaming murder at the Kilkenny man.

The game ended shortly after that and Galway had won.

Their supporters, mad with joy at their county's victory, swarmed like ants on to the pitch. Festy was lifted shoulder high and carried to the platform where the cup was being presented.

His team mates clapped him on the back and thanked him for saving the game for them.

"Ah, don't thank me," he told them. "I had nothing to do with it. It was the fairies."

They roared with laughter at this, but Festy was looking towards the canal end where a frock-coated fairy in a wide-brimmed hat hobbled painfully over the terrace steps and out of the ground.

Gerard Woulfe

Gypsy

Gypsy came into the house before Danny Murray was born. She hung on the wall above the battered old piano with the yellow keys. Danny didn't like her cross face when he was little. Sometimes when he did his piano practice he climbed up on the stool and turned the picture to the wall so that she couldn't listen.

Gypsy had thin red lips under a crooked big nose. Her eyelids were always half-closed in a sly sort of way – as if to hide what she was really thinking. The pearls round her neck looked like blobs of paint from close-up, but when you stepped back they caught the light, and glowed. Like magic, really. Gypsy was so real that Danny used to wonder whether she was still alive somewhere in the world.

One day Catherine Parr from down the street came into the house and she said that Gypsy's lips were red because she ate poisonous berries. She stuck out her tongue at Gypsy and she made Danny do the same.

When Danny was nine Gypsy got him into trouble. He climbed up on the piano stool and tried to give her a shave with his Daddy's razor and wobbling brush, but his mother came into the room at the wrong moment, and caught him in the act.

"Oh my glory!" she said. Mountains of creamy lather stood out from Gypsy's chin like snowcapped mountains on a map of the world. An avalanche of snow had blocked up her long, Roman nose.

"Danny Murray! Oh, I will murder you, you bad article. Brian – come you in here this minute, he's shaving *Gypsy*!"

His Daddy arrived, breathless, and did some staring at Gypsy's altered face.

"What are you playing at? Are you stupid? The only thing in the house that could be worth a fortune, and what do *you* do with it? Give it a blasted *shave*!"

And so Danny found himself driven up the stairs by the flat of his father's hand. That was the first time he realised that Gypsy might not be just any old picture. In some mysterious way, maybe she was worth something.

About this time Dr Moore began to call at the house to examine Danny's father, who wasn't feeling well. During one of these visits the doctor happened to notice Gypsy.

"Mrs Murray," he said, peering through his bushy eyebrows, "I have to remark on that dark-skinned beauty on your wall. Now that's what I call a proper

picture! Where did you get her – did you pick her up cheap at one of the auctions?"

"No, sure we've had that for years," said Danny's mother. "Maggie O'Brien and her man lit out for Canada and they auctioned all their stuff at the front door. My grandfather bought the picture and her mangle for two and six."

Dr Moore smiled, and repeated, "Two and six!" as he turned the painting over in his hands. "Pity it's not signed. But look at this canvas, I'd say this wasn't done by one of your weekend artists. Did you ever think of selling her?"

"Ah no," said his mother, turning a bit red. "Brian says we couldn't sell our luck."

"Well now – give me the first refusal," said Dr Moore, who aimed a massive wink at Danny as he put his stethoscope on Gypsy's chest and pretended to be deafened by the noise of her insides.

After that Danny's parents talked about Gypsy as if she was money in the bank. His Daddy used to say that he was going to sell Gypsy and buy a yacht and keep it in the harbour at Ballyholme. His mother wanted a house in the country with chickens and a goat. "How Will We Spend Gypsy" became a favourite family game. Then, when Danny turned eleven, his father died, and of course everything changed.

The Headmaster said special prayers for Danny in Assembly one morning. People were sorry for him because his Daddy had gone away to Heaven, and indeed, he was sorry for himself and for his Mummy. It was a long time before she did many of her ordinary things about the house, such as play the old piano in the living room. Then one day she played and made Danny sing that stupid song about Paddy McGinty's goat, and Danny felt good. They bought a black labrador pup and they had trouble teaching it not to widdle everywhere.

Danny noticed another change that came over his life at this time: there was no money to spend now that they had to live on what his Mummy earned. Sometimes he remembered the day when he bought three bars of Caramilk in the sweetie shop and ate them one after another on the way to school.

"You are one greedy spoiled pig, Danny Murray," Catherine Parr had told him, just because he only gave her two squares.

Now, times had changed. Catherine Parr was able to go on the school trip to Brittany, but Danny's mother sat down and cried when he told her what it would cost. Even when she became Manageress of the laundry where she worked on the Newtownards Road, still she complained that he grew too fast and ranted about the awful things he could do to a pair of shoes.

"I am going to buy you a pair of wooden Dutch clogs, Danny Murray," she used to say.

His mother was very friendly with the woman who owned the local fruit, vegetable and flower shop. This lady, Miss Finlay, gave Danny a job after school on Fridays and all day Saturdays. He spent most of the time sweeping the floors and making up delivery boxes. One afternoon Danny was wrapping an old newspaper round six big earthy leeks when an interesting headline caught his eye:

Fortune In The Attic

A County Antrim farmer learned yesterday that the painting found in his attic could be worth as much as £80 000.

"I'm only flabbergasted," he told our reporter. "It's been up there for years, I nearly threw it out. I don't even like it, you know – I like pictures with horses in them."

When asked what he was going to do with his windfall, Mr Cowan said, "Enjoy it!"

Danny began to think. If his Mummy had £80 000 she wouldn't have to scrimp and save or worry about the price of shoes. He thought of Gypsy's sly, hooded eyes; of the fine, strong jaw he'd once tried to shave; of the pearls round her neck and how they seemed to

glow from within if the light was right. Only a good artist could paint like that, even Dr Moore had said so.

How much, he wondered, was Gypsy really worth?

"Daniel Murray," called Miss Finlay from the front of the shop, "what's keeping those leeks – are you growing them, or what?"

That very evening, Danny made a point of sitting with his mother while she did some ironing. From time to time she wet the clothes with vapour from a plastic spray.

"Mummy."

"U-huh?"

"Miss Finlay says if you take a picture into a shop near the City Hall, they'll tell you what it's worth."

"Is that a fact, Danny."

"What would you buy if we sold Gypsy?"

For a moment or two, no answer came. His mother squeezed a squirt of misty water over the collar of a shirt.

"I couldn't sell Gypsy, I've had her since I was a wee girl."

"But if you *did* sell her, what would you buy?"

"A cuckoo clock!" said his mother, aiming a squirt of water at him. "Now run away out and play."

Two more weeks went by, bringing the end of term

and the start of the Easter holidays. Danny was bored in the house on his own. Most of his best friends were away with the school to Brittany and it didn't help him to think what a great time they must all be having over there. On Tuesday afternoon he came back from walking the dog in the Ormeau Park, and made a decision that set his blood racing.

He gently lifted Gypsy from the wall, put her into a large carrier bag, and caught a bus into town.

The journey into the centre of Belfast seemed to take about two minutes, for Danny's mind would not be still when he thought of what might happen in the next half hour. Goodbye Mr Scrimp and Mr Save. His mother might even give up her job! They could both fly out to see Uncle Robert in New Zealand or buy a house in the country and keep chickens and a car. Danny could think of dozens of ways of spending Gypsy, even if she wasn't worth quite as much as eighty thousand pounds.

He walked down Wellington Place and stood outside the shop with his heart beating like an engine, urging him on. His blood quickened, but his mind refused to be driven and he could not move. His mother would have a fit if she saw him right now! Danny closed his eyes and swallowed, thinking nervously how this was a bit like getting into the cold sea at Millisle. He took the plunge and went right in.

He was the only customer in the cool and very quiet gallery. The central area of the shop was fairly dim compared with the walls, which were illuminated by strips of fluorescent lighting. Some of the pictures hanging there were so huge that they made Gypsy look like a puny little thing – and to his amazement, Danny saw some very fancy carpets hanging on the walls. "Funny place to keep your carpets," he was thinking when a voice spoke.

"Yes? What do you want?"

The man who now approached wore a shabby Aran jumper. Using his fingers as a rake, he shifted his long grey hair away from his face.

"I've got a picture here," said Danny. "Could you tell me please if it's worth anything?"

"Another one. All right, let's take a look at it."

The man fitted glasses over his nose as he carried Gypsy a little closer to the window. He tapped the canvas with his fingernail and turned her over to examine the back just as Dr Moore had done all those years ago. Danny wanted to tell him some interesting things about his picture – how her name was Gypsy, that they'd had her for years and years, how she was supposed to be lucky – but he didn't have time. The man whipped the glasses off his face.

"This painting has no commercial value whatsoever.
The frame might fetch a penny or two if it was
competently restored, but the work itself . . . ? Most
likely a student's copy. No."

Danny accepted back his picture without speaking.
No commercial value. A copy. That final word fell
on his ears like a blow – No. He swallowed hard,
gathering his courage, wanting to strike back.

"But . . . didn't you see her pearls?"

"I saw her pearls."

Gypsy. How it destroyed him to think she wasn't even worth a cuckoo clock.

"But how do you *know*? How do you know she isn't worth anything?"

"Look, son," said the man, "what's your name?"

"Danny Murray."

"Right. Suppose that twenty or thirty women lined up outside this shop and one of them was your mother. And they all shouted 'Danny Murray' one after another. Do you think you'd know your mother's voice, could you pick it out from the others?"

"Probably."

"Well that's how it is with paintings. You know your mother's voice when you hear it because you're an expert on that topic. A great and valuable painting is like an old friend – an expert like me can pick it out immediately. Now go home, and take that Gypsy with you. A painting doesn't have to be worth money to be valuable."

Away he went into a far corner of his shop, leaving Danny to shove Gypsy into the carrier bag any old way, as if he was ashamed of her now that she was just plain cheap, and angry with her for making a fool out of him.

I hate that man! he thought as he crossed the road at Bedford Street lights, I hate him and his stupid shop and I hate his stupid carpets on his stupid walls.

How Will You Spend Gypsy? The game was over. Perhaps his mother had known all along. And Dr Moore. His Daddy, too. Maybe I was the only one who believed in Gypsy, thought Danny. The whole business filled him with such a deep, vague sadness that he wanted to be very, very young again.

When he got home his mother said, "And where have you been to, my lad! And just be careful what you say because I think I know."

"Mummy I just took it into that shop."

"Did you! Well you had no business taking it anywhere, give it to me, here."

She examined the picture carefully for signs of damage, and seemed satisfied.

"And what did they say in that shop?"

"I didn't go in," Danny said quickly. "I hadn't the nerve. Well, it was a big shop."

All of a sudden his mother giggled, and gave him a peck on the cheek.

"Ah dear love you, sure you're only young."

She fitted the picture over the lighter patch of wallpaper that marked the spot, and said, "There you are now, Gypsy," as if things were more or less back to normal.

Sam McBratney

The Hordes of Hell

The tinkling hand-bell and the voice of Brother Ardal called the monks to matins. Sherón had already risen. He stood in the centre of the hut, tightening the cincture about his tunic.

Brother Ardal gave the morning blessing in Latin: "Let us bless the Lord."

"May Jesus Christ be praised," Sherón answered, also in Latin.

He threw his cloak over his shoulders, fastening it with bronze pin and ring. The early October morning was cold, but he did not put on the leather sandals which lay by the foot of his bed. It was more virtuous to walk in bare feet and endure the cold of the flat stones paving the path to the oratory.

As yet there was little light. The monks came from clusters of huts in the eastern and western parts of the enclosure. Dim white figures in homespun cloaks, they shuffled along the paths of flat stones which criss-crossed the ground. All heads were bowed in prayer.

The rule ordained silence until after matins, so they did not greet each other when they met.

The oratory was bright, lit by a dozen rush-lights held in brackets along the side walls. The lights

flickered and the white cloths which draped the timber
walls stirred in the gentle breeze coming through the
open door.

When Sherón entered, only a few of the twenty
brothers had arrived. They sat on long benches, each
brother in his accustomed place, head bowed, hands
joined on his lap.

At the end furthest from the door was the altar, a
plain table of thick hewn oak; behind the altar, against
the backcloth, a crucifix. To the right a lectern stood,
and on it a psalter was open at the psalm which would

begin the matins service.

It was Sherón himself who had made the psalter in the monastery scriptorium. Before he joined the community, he had intended to enter a Bardic School and become a poet. Now he served God as a scribe, copying the scriptures and the writings of the early fathers of the Church.

Sherón saw that he was the only one whose feet were bare. All the others wore sandals, and a few had wrapped their legs and feet in thick woollen cloth.

"They're getting soft," he thought.

The abbot, who knelt nearest the altar at the right-hand side, nodded to the brothers at the opposite side. They began to chant the first psalm as all present rose to their feet. It was the custom that the two sides took turns in chanting the psalms.

Sherón studied the others as they sang. Some were finding it difficult to keep their eyes open. Others pulled comical faces as they tried to fight yawns. A few yawned openly.

"No discipline," Sherón said to himself. "Even if their sleep has been broken three times during the night to recite nocturns, they should by now be able to control sleeping and waking so that they do not come tired to matins.

"Should be given a day or two on bread and water.

As they ate, Brother Caffar read from St Jerome's *Life of Saint Paul of Thebes*, of his self-denial and penance in the wilderness.

Sherón ate none of the vegetables or fish on the table. He confined himself to bread and water, a self-imposed penance for lack of Christian charity in his thoughts about the brothers.

At the end of the meal he had come to a decision. He went to the abbot who had just risen from his place at table.

"I wish to speak with you, Father Abbot," Sherón said.

"Then speak, Brother Sherón."

"It is a matter on which I would prefer to speak in private, Father."

"Then come to my cell after vespers. I shall speak with you then, Brother Sherón."

After vespers Sherón stood waiting at the door of the abbot's hut.

"Enter, Brother," came the abbot's voice from within.

He sat on an oak chair near the only window in the rectangular hut. He beckoned Sherón to a stool, and the monk sat down facing him.

"I wish to leave the monastery, Father," Sherón said. "I seek your approval and your blessing."

The abbot did not speak for a while. The light from the window fell on the right side of his face, on his clear skin, on the high dome of his forehead and the line of white hair circling his head in the ear-to-ear tonsure. The left side of his face was in shadow.

"Why do you wish to leave us, my son?" Abbot Bercan asked gently.

"I wish to serve God in solitude, Father."

"I am sure, Brother Sherón, that you have given this matter much thought, and that anything I can say will not persuade you to stay among us."

"That is so, Father Abbot."

"Then go with my blessing, my son. The community and I will be without your fine example, your strength of purpose, your wise counsel. Many of us look upon you as a leader. The brothers believe that you will succeed me as abbot."

"Even if I were remotely worthy of that honour, Father, I could not assume the burden. I want to spend all my waking hours in contemplation of the Almighty. To set my mind to ordering the life of this monastery would prevent me from doing that."

"You are fortunate, my son, in being able to choose your way of serving God. Many of us serve him in answer to his call. In his mysterious way he has called us, and in humility we have answered.

"He may yet summon you, Sherón, and it is my prayer for you that, when he does, you will answer him with a generous heart."

Sherón left the monastery on the following day. He carried a leather satchel containing a few utensils, a knife, a wooden spoon, and a loaf of bread. These and the clothing on his back were his only worldly possessions.

After matins the brothers gathered at the gate of the enclosure to bid him farewell. Each came in turn and placed his hands on Sherón's shoulders. They looked into his eyes, but only Brother Ernin, the cellarer, spoke to him.

"Will you not think again, Sherón?" he asked. "We shall be lost without you."

Sherón shook his head and smiled.

"I shan't be cut off completely from you," he told Brother Ernin. "Father Abbot has insisted that I receive a visit from one among you at least once in every two weeks. I have promised to accept gifts of food from the monastery to add to what I can collect in the forest and on the shore. In a way I shall be part of the community still."

Sherón looked back when he was about to pass through the outer gate. They stood where he had left them, and, as he turned, they raised their hands in farewell.

"Oh, they are so good, so helpless, so innocent," he thought. "More and more I have felt it my duty to help them to cope with a world that is far from good or innocent, to protect them from the lies and trickery of the laymen in the outer enclosure, from the greed and thievery of the poor, and of those who accept the hospitality of the guest house."

Already, as he turned westward and walked along the river bank, he felt a great sense of freedom. He caught a glimpse of the dark river water through the sallows lining the bank. It gurgled continuously around reeds and water-lilies, and once he heard the screech of a moorhen and the sound of its wings slapping the water as it scuttled across its surface.

Leaving the river on his right, he walked through the herd of cattle grazing the clearing between the wood and the outer rath of the monastery. The oakwood was ringed with birch and hazel in autumn dress, all brown and yellow. A squirrel darted through the branches of a lone pine at the edge of the wood.

Sherón went into the half dark among the trees and followed a ferny path, well worn by deer and boar, and probably by cattle straying from the monastery herd. He heard some creature rustle dead leaves. A boar, perhaps, feeding on mast which littered the forest floor at that time of year.

The path climbed upward through the wood and emerged at the top of a high cliff. When Sherón came out of the wood at the cliff-top, he clambered down to a wide ledge about a tree-length below the top. Below him a sheer wall of rock dropped to where, on that calm day, the sea washed gently against the foot of the cliff. In the rock face at the level of the ledge was a narrow opening into a shallow cave, and this was the place Sherón had chosen to be his home.

It was another beautiful day. The sun had passed its noon and had begun to climb down the sky. The sea was as smooth as Sherón had ever seen it. A small cloud to the south was reflected in the still blue water. A gentle breeze wrinkled the reflection for a moment, but then it had gone by and all was serene again. Away out to sea a gull called and its cry carried clearly to Sherón.

Then to the east he saw a black dot on the water. He stood and shaded his eyes with his hand, trying to determine what it was. The black dot grew bigger. Then it was a beetle with about sixteen legs on each side of its body, all moving together as it crawled across the water. The legs moved to a regular rhythm, and each time they stepped on the water they raised white puffs of foam.

Nearer, it was a boat, huge by comparison with the naomhógs used by the community to fish the estuary. It was built of long, hewn planks overlapping and curved to a graceful, wave-cutting bow. A tall mast bearing a wide-striped sail, was set a little to the rear of mid-way. The sail was furled on the yard-arm in the calm weather. A tall figure stood by the mast and shouted orders in a strange language. The ship was heading for the estuary.

Sherón peeped around the edge of the cave-opening as the long boat came closer. There were about forty men on board. Two leaned over the gunwale near the prow. They looked towards the land, heads turning to left and right, examining the shore. They were jabbering excitedly.

All but a few of the oarsmen shipped oars. They stood up and began to buckle on shields. One man took weapons from a space under some loose planks near the centre and handed them around to the others. They looked fierce as they pulled on battered helmets and practised cutting and stabbing with sword and spear.

"Oh my God, have mercy upon us!" Sherón cried. "The monastery! They will attack the brothers."

As the boat, with just four men rowing, eased through the river mouth, Sherón dashed from the cave and ran through the wood, hoping he could warn the monks in time.

The wood was alive with people: monks and laymen scurried among the trees, all fleeing from the monastery. The abbot was there, stumbling along, carrying a great load in his cloak. Sherón knew from the clink of metal that he was taking the precious altar vessels to safety.

"How did you know they were coming?" Sherón asked him.

"The swineherd warned us. He saw them while they were still out to sea. Come on, Sherón. There is nothing you can do now. Flee for your life."

But Sherón did not go with him. He wanted to
know the fate of the monastery. When he came to the
edge of the wood, he climbed a high oak so that he
could see into the enclosure.

Already the longboat had been moored near the
monastery gate. The warriors had jumped ashore and
were storming through the outer gate. Sherón could
see them quite clearly and hear their furious yelling.

The inner gate was closed and they attacked it, hacking at it viciously with axes. Sherón could hear the sound of splintering timber. In a moment the gate was down and they charged through.

They scampered about the inner enclosure, shrieking like demons. A few went into the main oratory. The precious vessels had been removed by the abbot. They must have been disappointed and enraged at finding the place empty. They came out again.

A tiny puff of smoke rose from the roof of the oratory. Then another, and in a short while clouds of white smoke billowed upward. The smoke was followed by little spurts of flame flickering out the open door and between the planks of the wall. Then the whole building was swallowed in flames.

Other raiders went into the scriptorium and came out throwing things to the ground and beating and stabbing at them with their weapons. Sherón guessed that their beloved books were being mutilated by the villains. Smoke and flames then poured from the scriptorium.

The old church suffered the same fate; then the school. They went into the guest house, but they came out again immediately. To Sheron's horror they were dragging old Brother Ernin by his white hair. A yell of triumph rang out, and others ran to join in the sport.

They surrounded him, and Sherón could only imagine how they treated him from the flurry of movement and the manic squawking of his captors. Whatever his fate, his torment was brief. Almost immediately the devils dispersed among the monks' huts, leaving the old man huddled on the ground where he had fallen.

Soon all the huts were ablaze; then the huts in the outer enclosure. A thick cloud of smoke mushroomed over the whole monastery, and Sherón could no longer see what was happening. The attackers continued to shout and some of them began to cough in the smoke.

In the end they rushed out the gate and boarded the boat. The oars were manned and they rowed away.

Sherón went back to his hermitage to watch them leave. As they pulled out from the shore an evening breeze sprang up and they raised the broad-striped sail. It filled and bore the ship quickly and smoothly towards the east. The singing and harsh laughter of the marauders faded as they moved away.

When they had gone out of sight, Sherón went down through the wood again. The ruined monastery lay before him. The buildings were mere heaps of ashes with thin threads of smoke curling up from them. A few white-robed figures were moving about near the ruins of the oratory.

When Sherón arrived, there were just five brothers. Two of them were tapping with spades the mound of earth over a fresh grave. The others stood by with bowed heads, dejected.

"Brother Ernin," said one pointing at the earth.

"I know," Sherón said. "Let us pray for him."

A few minutes went by as each monk prayed in silence, eyes downcast. They were stunned by what had happened. It was the end of the world as they had known it.

"The abbot told us to go to the monastery at Killnaleck," Brother Fiach told Sherón. "Most of the others have gone there. The lay workers and their families have gone too."

"You will follow them now," Sherón suggested.

For a long time there was no answer.

"This is our home," Brother Rúan said eventually, his voice shaking with sorrow.

"I am twenty-five years here," said Brother Cainnech. "My life is here."

"What's to become of us?" Brother Tiarnach asked in a fearful whisper.

"You could try to build it up again," Sherón told them. "But I cannot stay with you. I must return to

my cave on the cliff. My life is there now."

They were silent.

"God be with you, brothers," Sherón said and turned away.

Though his back was to them, he sensed the sadness in their eyes. They were like lost sheep, and he knew they could not survive without a shepherd.

"However, it is my destiny to serve God in solitude in the wilderness," he assured himself.

As he was passing through the gateway, a faint voice called: "Sherón, please don't leave us."

He stood still.

What was it the abbot had said? Something about answering with a generous heart.

He turned and walked slowly back to them.

"Let us get to work, my brothers," he said gruffly. "First of all we must remove those ashes. We'll put them in the garden. We shall dig them in with the clay in the springtime to help the new growth."

Gerard Woulfe

The Wooing of Emer

The sunbower of Emer, daughter of Fergal Monach,
was of white wickerwork interwoven with purple and
red. The furniture was of polished ashwood, carved
and gilded, and strewn with cushions of stitched
crimson leather. All day long the air was filled with
the cooing of doves and the laughter of women. And
Fergal Monach, who was King in the West, sat within
his great hall surrounded by his poets, his champions
and his councillors.

At that time, Conchubair Mac Neassa was High
King in Ulster. And his court there, was the wonder of
the world. First among the champions of the High
King was Cú Chulainn who was called The Hound of
Ulster. War bands fled at the sight of his chariot and
brave men fell to the ground at the sound of his war
cry. And no man in Ireland dared to face his battle
frenzy.

Bards and poets and storytellers passed from house
to house and from hill to hill and down dusty roads to
the courts of kings. And Cú Chulainn heard of the
beauty and the charm and the skills of Emer, the
daughter of Fergal Monach. And Emer heard of the
beauty and the strength and the skills of the Hound
of Ulster.

Servants whispered in the house and rumour passed
in the woods and word came to Fergal Monach that
Cú Chulainn was coming into his land to woo his
daughter. And Fergal Monach swore that no man of
Ulster would have claim to the lands to the West. But
Emer sat in her sunbower and laughed and waited.

Then Fergal Monach came to Ulster bringing with
him gifts and gold for the High King. And he asked
if it were true that Cú Chulainn who was called the
Hound of Ulster was in his service. And the High
King said that he was the best of his warriors.

"I have heard it said," said Fergal Monach, "that
if Cú Chulainn had studied the skills of war under
Scáthach, the Warrior Witch of Alba, he would excel
all the warriors of the world."

"There is no warrior in the world who excels him
now," said the High King.

"But he has not learned what Scáthach has to
teach," said Fergal Monach. "So those whom she
has taught excel him now."

Then Cú Chulainn faced the company. A tall, fair
boy, arrogant and watchful. A purple, five-folded
tunic about him. A brooch of inlaid gold on his white
breast. And Cú Chulainn spoke and his eyes did not
leave the eyes of the stranger, the king of the West.

"Fergal Monach," said the Hound of Ulster, "I will

go into Alba and learn what Scáthach has to teach a warrior. And I will not die there. I will come back to your land in the West, Fergal Monach. And I will have your daughter.''

Grey rain was falling on a grey beach when Cú Chulainn came to Alba. He entered into the hall of bronze where Scáthach sat on her seat of iron.

Then Cú Chulainn moved as an otter moves through water and the blade of his sword was between the witch's breasts.

"Your wishes from me, Hound of Ulster," said Scáthach. "Your wishes as you utter them in one breath."

And Cú Chulainn opened his mouth and spoke in one breath.

"The feats of a warrior from you, Scáthach, The Apple Feat, The Thunder Feat, The Blade Feat, The Spear Feat, The Rope Feat, The Body Feat, The Cat's Feat, The Salmon Feat, The Throw Of The Staff, The Wheel Feat, The Breath Feat, The Hero's Whoop, The Blow, The Counter Blow, The Running Up The Lance And Righting The Body On Its Point, The Scythe Chariot and the Hero's Twisting Round The Points Of Spears."

Then Scáthach rose from her iron seat and her voice was the voice of iron.

"You will learn them," she said, "those feats and countless others. And when you have learnt all that Scáthach has to teach, Hound of Ulster, hosts will flee from the sound of your voice and no man will walk before you in the courts of the kings of the world."

So Cú Chulainn joined the scholars of Scáthach. And Scáthach knew that his deeds would still be sung when she and her scholars had passed away and long been forgotten.

In Fergal Monach's fort in the West servants whispered and women gathered in corners and warriors looked to the North. And pedlars and packmen and horse traders and cattle traders carried the news. And beggarmen in the kitchens mumbled it into their bowls of milk. And all the stories were the same story; that Cú Chulainn had returned to the court of the High King. And Fergal Monach stopped up his ears and would not hear the whispering.

Then, one morning, Emer spoke to her women. "Let one of you go out now and see what you can see."

There was a balcony of oakwood outside the sunbower and a carved rail around it. And the woman put her hand on the rail and looked into the North. And she called to Emer within.

"Two steeds I see of like size, beauty, fierceness and speed. I see a chariot of fine wood and wickerwork on which are white bronze wheels. A man there is in the chariot, the fairest of the men of Ireland. A purple, five folded tunic is about him, a brooch of inlaid gold at his white breast."

And Emer sat in her sunbower and laughed. "It is Cú Chulainn," she said. "It is the Hound of Ulster. I will have him."

Felicity Hayes-McCoy

A Night in the Grand Hotel, Gortnaskeagh

Tom O'Brien stood by the wall of McCarthy's shop.
To the people of the remote village of Gortnaskeagh
he was as much part of the scene as the clock over the
community centre or the pump at the centre of the
village square. Standing there, mighty in his garda
uniform, he was their bulwark against the wickedness
of the world.

He liked the evening time best, when the place grew
quiet. At twilight a few villagers strolled around the
square, chatting and glancing at the shop windows.
They exchanged a few words with Tom as they went
by. Traffic was light, just an occasional car flashing its
headlights as it passed. It was time to 'tuck the town
in' as he put it.

But first he had to see the bus arrive from Killarney.
For a short time after its arrival in the square, the
sleepy village stirred into life. People got out of the
bus and walked across the square and turned right or
left into the village street. It was all one street, but
roughly at its mid point it widened into the square.

Some passengers went to cars which were parked all
day in the square, got into them and drove away. Tom

knew them all. There were two strangers, however, who hurried into the hotel. Not many villages of its size could boast a hotel, but Gortnaskeagh was a well-known angling centre. Some of the best fishing in the country was available in the rocky pools of the Owgarriff river, especially in a five mile stretch close by the village.

The street lights came on and the light was lit in the public house at the corner. The village was sinking back into sleep. There was only the muffled sound of talk and laughter from the pub, and somewhere across the valley a dog was barking.

Tom set off on his end-of-day patrol. He sauntered down one side of the street and up the other. All was as it should be. He checked the door of the post office and the shutters on its windows. Earlier that day he had supervised the delivery of cash for pensions and children's allowances. He had seen it stacked in the safe in neat bundles tied with paper bands.

"I wonder," he muttered to himself as he went around to check the back of the building.

He strolled back to the square and went into the hotel.

"Good night, Maeve," he greeted the receptionist.

"Hi, Tom," she answered pleasantly. "What brings you here?"

Tom leaned a hip against the edge of the desk and looked around. The entrance hall was deserted save for the two of them.

"How's your father?" he asked Maeve. "I haven't seen him in a while."

"Oh, he's fine," said the girl, and she smiled at Tom. "But my father's health isn't worrying you now. Is it, Tom?"

Tom ignored her question and gazed at the floor.

"Busy?" he asked.

"Not very. Just the usuals and two strangers."

"Is that so?" Tom asked. "The two strangers, now. Where are they from?"

"They gave Cork as their home address," she told him, and she turned the hotel register around so that he could read it.

The last two names were John Murphy and James Barry, both from Cork; date of arrival, 3rd June, and date of intended departure, 4th June. They were in Room 12.

"They are leaving again in the morning," Tom said. "Did they order a taxi?"

"No, but they asked what time the bus left for Killarney."

"And did they not think 7.30 a bit early?"

"No. They seemed to be quite happy about it."

"What luggage did they have?"

"They had two large suitcases – one each," Maeve told him.

"No fishing gear?" Tom asked, his eyebrows raised in a question.

"No, unless it was in the cases."

"Strange," Tom murmured. "Very strange!"

"What's strange, Tom?"

"Just one night in the Grand Hotel, Gortnaskeagh. No fishing gear. Arriving at 9.30 p.m., departing at 7.30 a.m. the following morning. Don't you think that's strange?"

Outside the hotel door Tom paused. He lifted his cap and scratched his head. Then he seemed to make up his mind about something. He walked boldly along the side of the square, round the corner to the post office.

He knocked at the side door. A voice within asked: "Who is it?"

"It's me, Tom O'Brien. Open up, Dick. I want to have a word with you."

Five minutes later Tom came out of the post office.

"Remember now," he said to Dick Clancy, the postmaster, "don't go near the shop. It's only money and not worth taking risks for. But at the slightest sound in the shop switch the light in your bedroom on and off, just once. I'll be watching from across the street, in Ned Whelan's and I'll take it from there.''

He went across the street and knocked at Whelan's door.

''May I come in, Nellie?'' he asked when the door was opened.

Night time is quiet in small villages far from the big towns and cities. Gortnaskeagh is like a ghost town after dark. Sounds of gaiety came from the public house at the corner, but in the open nothing moved. Later the street came alive for a short while as people went home noisily from the pub. Then it was silent.

In the houses lights went out one by one. A dog wandered around the street, sniffing at walls and

scraps of litter lying on road and footpath. Then he too was gone and there was nothing, nothing but circles of lamplight outside the sleeping houses.

At about half past one the light flashed in Dick Clancy's bedroom. Seconds later Whelan's door opened and Tom O'Brien came out. He tip-toed up the street and round the corner to the hotel.

He burst through the twin glass doors at the entrance, startling Paddy Lynch, the night porter, who was nodding in his chair at the desk.

"The fellows in Room 12, Paddy," Tom said quickly. "Did they go out?"

"I don't think so, Tom. They didn't pass through here since I came on duty anyway," the porter said.

"Come on," said Tom as he hurried towards the stairs. "Bring the keys to Number 12."

Paddy took his key ring and followed. When he arrived at the corridor running by the bedrooms, Tom was already standing at the door to Room 12. He had his ear against the door, listening. Paddy wondered how one of his size could have got there so quickly.

Tom knocked at the door. No answer. He knocked again. Still no answer.

"Open it," he told Paddy.

They went into the room, Tom in the lead. It was in complete darkness save for the faint grey rectangle of the window in the wall opposite the door. They stood there for a few moments, listening carefully.

"Nobody here," Tom remarked as he groped for the light-switch behind the door. He turned on the light. A quick glance around told him all he needed to know: two suitcases on a bed, one of them open and empty, the lower sash of the window raised and the hooks of a rope ladder gripping the sill.

Tom switched off the light at once.

"Now, Paddy, go down to your desk and sit there as if nothing had happened. I'll call you on the phone when I want you."

"What's going on, Tom?" the porter asked.

"I haven't time to tell you now, Paddy. Will you just do as I ask, please."

"All right, Tom."

When Paddy had gone, Tom closed the door and felt his way to a wardrobe which stood by the window. He had seen in the fleeting moment while the light was on that between the wardrobe and the wall there was a space which was out of view of the rest of the room. He stepped into this space and waited.

In the silence the slightest sound was magnified: a creaking board in a room near by, a flutter of curtain stirring in the soft breeze through the open window. Once he was startled by a sudden clatter of tin cans in the hotel yard below the window. The silence which followed seemed deeper than ever.

"A cat raiding the rubbish bin," he told himself.

Then suddenly he was alert, every sense, and especially his hearing, on edge. What was it? A sound so faint that he was not quite sure he had heard it. But yes; there it was again. It came from the window. The points of the rope-ladder hooks tensed and moved imperceptibly as the ladder took the weight of a climber.

Tom held his breath. He could hear the scrape of a toecap on the wall. A man stepped into the room. His comrade soon joined him, and they pulled up the rope ladder.

"Close the window very quietly now, Jack," one said.

"You draw the curtain, Bill, and I'll switch on the light," said the other man.

Tom blinked as the light came on, but he did not move. The men went to one of the beds, and the one called Jack emptied the contents of a black calico sack on the bedspread.

"Not a bad haul," his companion remarked.

Tom peeped around the front of the wardrobe. The men were standing with their backs to him, looking down at a heap of money on the bed. They were

dressed all in black – pants and polo-neck jumpers. As far as Tom could determine, their faces were blackened too.

"No amateurs here," he thought.

While they were intent on examining their loot, counting it and fondling it, Tom tip-toed carefully forward until he was standing just behind them. They had no idea that anyone else was in the room. Then, without warning, Tom shattered the silence of the night.

"GLORY CAPPAMORE!" he roared at them.

The effect was amazing. Both men turned around and stood stock still, as if paralysed, their mouths wide open. They looked so startled that Tom could scarcely refrain from laughing. When he produced handcuffs, they meekly offered him their wrists, and he handcuffed them together.

"Now sit there on the bed, boys," he told them, "and we'll invite a few guests."

Still dumb with surprise, they sat down. Tom picked up the phone on the bedside locker.

"Paddy," he said, "ring 999 and ask them to send a squad car. Then ring Dick Clancy. Ask him to check his safe and then to come over here. Tell him I want him to meet a few friends from out of town."

Gerard Woulfe

The Duel

The snowdrops were waving their white heads along
the paths as Major Macnamara's coach stopped in
front of Daniel O'Connell's house. The morning was
cold; the air said there would be snow but snow had
been threatening this past few days.

As the row had been getting hotter the weather had
been getting colder. 'The row' was what had brought
Major Macnamara. He hurried out of the coach, his
embroidered coat swinging around him, and he went
up to the door. Daniel O'Connell opened it as the
major came striding up the steps.

"Well?" he said.

"The challenge has arrived," said the major.

"And about time too," O'Connell said, trying to
avoid a tremble of excitement, maybe fear, in his
voice. He was glad that at last the whole affair was
coming to a head.

O'Connell was a lawyer, born in Kerry, living in
Dublin, who specialised in taking law cases for the
poor. He had gone to school in France during the
French Revolution. He had been there when the heads
were falling into baskets from the guillotines, the
bodies of nobles lying upside-down in ditches. He

knew of the killing in the streets and in the flat landscape around Paris. His own school had been ransacked by the rebels. He had come back to Ireland a trained lawyer, sure that the only way to settle differences was through the law and within the law. Yet the letter that his friend, the major, was handing to O'Connell now, was from a man called D'Esterre, challenging him to a duel.

He read it quickly:

> Mr O'Connell,
>
> It's now over a week since you said that the members of Dublin Corporation were a 'beggarly' lot. Since you still refuse to withdraw the word 'beggarly' I now, on behalf of the members of the Corporation, challenge you to a duel at a place and a time to be arranged between my agents and your . . . .

Major Macnamara was talking even as O'Connell was reading.

"If you ask me it's a conspiracy, and this D'Esterre is being used by people who want rid of you," he said. "You're too good a lawyer, too much in demand. They think you'll refuse the challenge and if you do you'll be so dishonoured that your word will be worth nothing and you'll be ruined. Thank God they've underestimated your resolve."

"What time did you tell them?" O'Connell asked.

The major, never one to smile, managed to curl his lip faintly.

"Half past three today."

"That soon?"

"In these winter days darkness falls early. I don't wish the waning light to make it into a thing of chance," said the major.

For a moment O'Connell stood without speaking. Then he said: "Are there other preparations? I'm not used to this business."

"I've sent for Bennett's pistols," said the major briskly. "They're the best; he's killed more men than anyone I know."

"Thank you."

"I've also asked a priest to hide in a nearby cottage in case...."

He stopped, wondering if he had already said too much.

"In case I fall," O'Connell said.

"Yes," said the major firmly. "But you won't. D'Esterre will be the one to fall."

"Except we both miss," O'Connell said.

"It won't be like that," the major said. "I wanted to limit it to one shot each but those clowns around D'Esterre wouldn't have it. 'Five and twenty shots,' they said. 'If it takes that many.' "

"So it's him or me," said O'Connell.

"D'Esterre wants to be a hero."

"Maybe I do too," said O'Connell. He stood a moment thoughtful.

"Where will it be?"

"In Bishopscourt in County Kildare. I have preparations to make and I'll see you there at three."

He left as briskly as he had come, the horses' hooves crunching the gravel as they turned to head down the avenue. There were a few spittles of sleety snow in the wind.

Alone now for a moment O'Connell's mind went back over the past week. It had been like a circus. After D'Esterre had written demanding the apology, O'Connell had written back saying he meant every word he said. Two more letters were exchanged on the Saturday, both of them couched in wild language. On Monday it was rumoured all around the city that D'Esterre was planning to meet O'Connell in Grafton Street, and horsewhip him; some people even went as far as hiring a room overlooking the street so that they could see the fun from the window. But D'Esterre never appeared. On Tuesday he marched his followers around the streets of Dublin chanting insults to

O'Connell. Later that evening O'Connell retaliated in kind. In the normal course, with all this going on, both of them would have been arrested. But they weren't. O'Connell suspected that somewhere there were people who wanted it to go to the death. If there was going to be a death, he vowed it wasn't going to be his.

Now it was Wednesday and things were moving quickly. O'Connell's brother came in and when he heard the news he went off to help the major with his arrangements. People began to cheer at the bottom of the avenue and some ventured in the gates to look up at the windows of the house for a glimpse of O'Connell. Coaches began heading out of the city towards Kildare and people on horseback stopped as they passed the house where O'Connell lived. 'The Vulture' Mahoney arrived trying to sell pistols. With his hooked nose and white ribbed hair it was easy to see why he got his name. And before O'Connell could tell him he didn't want any, the Vulture was already in full spate:

"Now I wouldn't recommend this one because it fires a couple of inches too high. Fine if you aim for his neck you'll get him between the eyes. But if you aim for his heart you'll only get him in the shoulder – the left one at that and since he's right-handed. . . . But this one here is a prize." He caressed the pistol with affection. "Every time I look at it I thank God for the hands he gave to man to make things of such beauty; the balance, the feel of it, the exact weight of the trigger. Take this, Mr O'Connell and you'll upend him before he has time to . . . . "

He left quickly when O'Connell told him he was well supplied and he headed off to try his luck with D'Esterre. The streets were alive with people talking about the duel: blacksmiths shouting to bakers about it, carpenters to shopkeepers, policemen trying desperately not to hear lest they should be expected to arrest the participants. People, with bread and pots of porridge to eat along the way, were heading out in slow carts along the south side of the Liffey.

In the afternoon the snow came whitening the streets and the road out to Bishopscourt. It didn't settle on the busy road but it sprinkled the fields and gave a pure look to the countryside which O'Connell was passing through. The people, now in gay mood, threw it playfully at each other. Some were taking bets on the outcome of the duel. Near Bishopscourt O'Connell's coach began to pass the local people who, attracted by the noise and the rumours, were hurrying to the hollow where the combat was to take place. They followed the coach-tracks to where the coaches

were lined up in rows along the road and followed the
tracks through the snow over the fields, across ditches.
O'Connell himself slipped as he crossed a ditch and
damp earth marked the lapel of his black coat. It was

something which worried the major when he saw it and he tried to wipe it off.

"It's only dirt," O'Connell said.

"Yes, but it gives him something to aim at. And take off that white tie and put on a black one; white is too easy to see in gunsights."

When he was changing ties, the Vulture, obviously unsuccessful with D'Esterre, came over to him.

"At least Mr O'Connell, you'll not have to suffer this rascal taunting you any more. Either you'll be dead tomorrow, God be good to you, or you'll be looked on as a hero. Whereas if you had let him off with it, you'd never be a liar."

"A liar?"

"What you are. One of them fellas in court."

"Are they liars?" O'Connell said, glad of the chatter to hide his anxiety.

"They're both lawyers and liars most of them. Because they be telling everybody to keep the law and fining them. And then they go out breaking it by duelling and killing. Sure half the judges around here wouldn't be judges at all if they hadn't killed off all the other barristers who could have got the job. That's why I think you're right, Mr O'Connell and I'll say a prayer for you if you're dead." Then he was off through the crowd, looking for a high piece of ground from which he could see everything.

The crowd, already becoming quiet with expectation, was beginning to settle in rows along the slopes. Major Macnamara took the pistols from his box and, in a calm voice, gave his last-minute instructions. He handed the pistol to O'Connell, a notch in the handle for every man it had killed. They walked together to the centre of the hollow and D'Esterre and he, without speaking, stood back to back. The referee came forward. The major and D'Esterre's second moved away. The crowd went silent as in a church.

The referee counted out the ten paces. They turned and fired. A gasp and then a cheer went up from the crowd as D'Esterre fell, blood spurting from a wound in the pit of his stomach. His second and his helpers ran to lift him hurriedly to the cart which would carry him to his coach. O'Connell saw the wound as he was being carried past and he knew that D'Esterre would bleed to death, if not tonight then in the next few days. He thought of his young wife and children and the grief which would be brought to them. The thought was banished when the major ran to congratulate him and the crowd surged in to shake his hand. He was slapped on the back, cheered, pushed and jostled. People struggled to get near him to tell him how glad they were that he had won. The white-haired figure with the hooked nose managed to get through the crowd and stand at his elbow.

"Now you're an honourable man," the Vulture was saying. "I can be proud to say I know you and from now on all them liars will think twice before they call you a bad barrister."

O'Connell knew that this was true but he wished the silliness would end. Pistols were becoming too accurate and duelling too dangerous. The price of honour, now in 1815, was becoming too high even for the winner. The long day was over and he was still able to see the moon beginning to rise over the trees and feel the frost which was about to harden the snow. But was it not too great a punishment for being a loud mouth that D'Esterre's body should already be getting weaker, his head swinging from side to side and groans of pain rising from his throat as the wheels trundled over the rutted cart-path? D'Esterre's horses thrust onwards, vibrant and throbbing with life, as they pulled the dying man's cart out of the hollow. Maybe, O'Connell thought, that was what was meant by horse-sense. Horses didn't kill each other for being brave fools.

John McArdle

Portrait of Daniel O'Connell

Daniel O'Connell (1775–1847) is a very important figure in Irish history in the first half of the nineteenth century. Having seen the French revolution at first hand as a young man, he hated political violence. In its place, he invented what is now known as 'street politics' or non-violent protest for political ends. O'Connell's duel with D'Esterre early in his career tells us much about the times he lived in, and may have been a crucial point in the formation of his character.

The episode also occurred at a crucial point in the history of duelling which lasted from about 1750 (with swords) until about 1835. The reason duelling ceased was that pistols had become too accurate and the risk was consequently too great. The story tries to give some insights into the pressures which led people into such a seemingly foolish pursuit.

Oyo's Cave

Once there lived on the Antrim coast a man called
Oyo. He was known as a very fine farmer. At harvest
time, when the barrels of grain were counted, the
yield from Oyo's field was always double that of his
neighbours. For three years running, the people
marvelled at Oyo's crops. They said that his success
was due to hard work, good luck, and well drained
land.

There was in those days a dry cave in one of the
coves, and it was said that this cave had magical
powers. The people believed that spirits inhabited the
cave, which explains why they marked the entrance
with a large white stone in case someone should
wander in by accident. It was well known how more
than one spirit lived in the forbidden place, and that
some of the spirits were benevolent, some downright
evil.

Each spring after sowing his seed, Oyo went secretly
to the cave with a bucket in each hand. Inside the cave
he took a stone and drew a picture of a wheatsheaf
on the roof. Always, when he did this, Oyo was in a
hurry, for the cave was dark and damp and filled with
the noises of creatures scuttling about.

Next morning at first light Oyo returned to the cave to see whether the spirits had granted him his wish, and found a sheaf of wheat lying on the floor of the cave. Of course this was a miraculous thing, for the season was Spring, yet the heads of these stalks were heavy with fat, pale-yellow seeds. In this way, the spirits told Oyo that his wish had been granted.

Oyo was a cunning man. He filled his two buckets with seaweed for the return journey to his cottage. He knew that if his neighbours saw him with the buckets, they would never guess that he had been to the cave of the spirits, but would say: "Look at Oyo, what a worker he is. He has been to the shore to collect seaweed to fertilise his crops."

Then came a time of great trouble, for there was no food. The river burst its banks and the land squelched underfoot and nothing flourished but mosses and wild rush. The grain crop failed everywhere, except for one place. On Oyo's land the stalks stood tall and strong.

As harvest time approached, Oyo was plagued by thieves. They came in the night with sickles and cut down portions of his crop even while the grain was still green and milky. That is a measure of the people's hunger at this time.

It soon became clear to Oyo that he would lose all of his crop if he did not act quickly. Yet what could he do?

Even a man of his strength could not resist people who were driven by hunger.

Oyo returned to the cave in the cove. This time, because he was about to make a special request, he concealed in his bucket a small clay pot into which he had dripped the blood of an animal, for it was common knowledge that a sacrifice sometimes stirred a lazy spirit into doing what was asked of it.

In the echoing darkness Oyo told the spirits that he wanted a beast to come and guard his crops. With a trembling hand he drew on the roof the sort of thing he had in mind. He gave his beast large pointed ears, so that it could hear people creeping in the night. He gave it a long jaw full of pointed teeth, and four legs so that it could run faster than a man. He also told the spirits that he wanted the creature to have a gruff voice, and that it was to do whatever he ordered. And he smeared a little of the blood from the clay pot on to the creature's tongue to be sure that his meaning was plain.

Oyo went to the cave early next morning, just before sunrise.

And there it was, as he had imagined it in almost every detail. Even the tongue drooping between white teeth was red as he had ordained. Oyo told the beast to sit, and it sat. He told it to speak, and it sounded out a

low, tremulous growl. Most pleasing of all, when Oyo left the cave, the beast followed meekly as if Oyo was its lord and master. He did not bother to fill his bucket with seaweed to go home, now that he had such a fearsome ally to protect him from the wrath of the people.

And so the mythical beast protected Oyo's crops from the hunger of the people. His neighbours, and the people from the glens who had been making thin porridge out of his wheat before it was ready, took one look at this thing with the mouthful of teeth and went grubbing for roots instead. One man, made braver than the rest by extreme hunger, tried to ignore the beast's growling temper, and returned to his settlement with torn flesh and teeth marks about his ankles and arms, and his example was enough. In the night, when the howl of the beast was heard throughout the land, the people trembled.

In this way the mythical beast was a wonderful help to Oyo.

But now see what happened! One day Oyo's young daughter wandered away from the cottage into the cornfield, where the yellowing stalks grew taller than her head. She did not see the creature that came darting towards her through the ripening corn, and her small bones were like straws in the mouth of the beast.

Her cries brought Oyo running, and he saw at once that he was too late. Oyo was weakened by his sorrow at such a dreadful happening, and yet he was also strengthened by his rage. He picked up sticks and stones and beat the animal about the head, whereupon it turned on him, too, and made him run.

He went at once to the settlement to tell what had happened.

"I see now," Oyo told his neighbours, "what a selfish fool I have been. I see now how much people need to stand by one another in time of trouble. Come with me now, help me kill this thing, and I will fill the bowl of every man, woman and child with grain from my own fields."

The men of the settlement left to hunt the beast down. They brought sticks and stones, and spears, and fire. The women came too, for they feared just as much as the men for the safety of their children if this creature should grow more angry, more fierce, and run wild.

The sticks and spears did not work. The mythical beast ignored them, and came on with short, menacing runs, snapping, growling, and clawing at the air. But some of the women had thought to bring nets with them, the strong sort used for landing large fish, and they trapped the beast in the nets, and killed it.

And now, Oyo lifted the body of his daughter in his arms and walked with her all the way down the Long Inch, and into the cove. Some people who were sympathetic to him offered to share the weight of the body, but Oyo would not be moved from doing this thing himself. He carried his daughter to the mouth of the cave of spirits, and went in.

On the roof of the cave he drew a picture of his daughter, and while the light of his torches burned

away, he laboured to make his drawing complete in every detail. And when it was finished, Oyo fell in the dirt on the floor of the cave and grovelled and begged as never before for this final favour.

Oyo kept a vigil outside the cave all through the night, and many of his neighbours sat with him. They waited for the sun to come up. Then Oyo went into the cave.

He came out with tears of pure joy running down his face, for his daughter was alive and holding her father's hand. You can easily imagine what a different mood there was among the people as they left the shore by way of the Long Inch, and returned to their settlement.

Two weeks later, Oyo brought his barrels of grain to a place of common ground overlooking Needle Rock. And he shared his crop equally among the families of the community.

You can still see the cave where Oyo drew the mythical beast on the roof. It looks as though it has been filled in by collapsing rock, but that is not what happened to it. The people went down to the cave and filled it in stone by stone so that it could never bring evil down on them again.

Sam McBratney

Statue of Pádraic Ó Conaire

If you have ever been to Galway and you have been to Eyre
Square in the centre of the town, you will have seen the statue of
a little man with a hat back on his head. He is Pádraic Ó Conaire,
author of dozens of stories in the Irish language. He was born in
1882, brought up in an Irish-speaking home in Connemara,
educated at Blackrock College and Rockwell College in Tipperary,
joined the British civil service and worked in London until 1914.
He came back to Connemara then and wandered around Connacht
telling stories, writing stories, being welcomed in houses and
being given a night's lodgings for the entertainment he gave in
those days before television.

He died in the Richmond Hospital, Dublin in 1928, at the age
of 46. When they searched for his belongings the only things he
had in the world were a pipe, some tobacco and an apple.

The Encounter was written in Irish as all his stories were. This
translation appeared in a book published in 1982 to commemorate
the centenary of his birth.

I was just about to reel in the line, give up the effort
of pretence and let the current be master of the boat
when I noticed the transformation which had come
upon my hound. I put out the oars to steady the boat
in the flow. What could be the matter with him? He
had come out about five yards from the bank and was
standing on a pile of sandy sediment which the reeds
had sifted from the stream. He was less than ten
yards from me, nose sniffing, ears cocked, eyes intent.
I whistled but he paid no attention to me or my
whistling. Every limb was tense, every sense on edge.
He was no longer the limpid companion of the
riverbank but as alive and sharp as any animal I had

ever seen, an arrow in a drawn bow. Suddenly it was as if the arrow were released and he thudded fast as sight into the water. The water churned and whisked along the sandy bank and by the time my eyes could make out what was happening the big red hunting-dog was scrambling around, wrestling with something in the scraggy water among the reeds.

Whatever it was was smaller than he but it struggled dreadfully. Mire and sand kicked up from the land-neck so that I could see in the thrashed water neither the hound nor the shape of his adversary. Only one could survive in such a fight. They turned and rolled and arched together; the strong wiry reeds shook and clattered against each other making a sound like the spines in the treetops of a wood tangling together in a windstorm.

The hound managed, after a long time, to wrench and drag the other animal ashore. By now it was difficult to make out his red hide, clogged as it was by the silt and sand. He had become the same colour as the spattered plunder in his stranglehold.

It was an otter. It feigned death as he hauled it in and, fooled by it, he let it fall from his grip on to the dry land. It turned quickly and made a dash on its short legs for the safety of the stream. But it wasn't quick enough and the hound pounced on it again.

Gaining strength from the fierceness of its nature and the danger it was in, the otter succeeded in twisting its broad low head around and sinking its teeth, short and sharp as pincers, into the hound's dark nose. Then taking advantage of the hound's momentary bewilderment, it released its grip and tried again to reach the water. But it couldn't make it. It squealed as the dog caught it by the throat and shook it venomously, the blood of the two animals mixing and blending together. He threw it into the air. He caught it again before it hit the ground. It squirmed and he jerked and shook it again till it seemed to me as I watched that both animals were on the point of exhaustion.

But the hound's strength was greater than that of the otter, his resilience like the switch-back of a sally. Suddenly he released his hold on it only to catch it again immediately. Over the heart this time. He sank his teeth in deep. Foam was coming from the mouths of the two of them, all strength teased from their limbs; you could hear their breathing in the quietness of the day; the slow racked panting of the two of them and, as the heaving of one faltered, you could hear, if your ear was sharp enough, the last pitiful weak-voiced squeak of the stream's native dweller. The kill was done.

The hound stood up on the pile of sand, thrust his nose into the air and let out a great howl of victory. It echoed through the shivering tops of the reeds and over the quiet stream, out towards where the shadows of the clouds flitted across the faces of the mountains. He was letting the world know that the ravaged being at his feet was dead and that he had done what his nature and his Maker intended he should do.

Barry Wilkinson

The Black Pig's Dyke

When Maeve was queen of Connacht there came a
year when rain poured all during the summer and the
sky was dark with clouds so that the grass couldn't be
made into hay and the corn in the fields was slow to
ripen. But in the next province of Ulster the weather
was bright and sunny and the wheat and corn was
golden in the fields around Ard Macha.

By August of that year the people knew that they
would not have enough food to do the winter and one
day Maeve and her soldiers rode their horses into
Ulster to take the grain which had just ripened in the
wide fields. A witch made them invisible and to the
eyes of the people of Ulster it seemed as if the corn
was lifting itself from the ground, beating itself against
stones till it was threshed. Then bags appeared out of
invisible carts and the grain poured itself into them.
Since the carts were invisible too, the people of Ulster
seemed to see the sacks gather themselves into piles
which floated a few feet above the ground and headed
off into the setting sun.

They were too afraid to follow them or try and stop
them, but the hatred of the people of Ulster became
so great that a witch woman came into the place from

which the most grain was taken and she changed the
white pigs in the fields into black pigs and she sent
them after the army of Maeve to avenge the theft
which had taken place.

Cheering greeted the queen and her men when they
arrived back in Connacht. Maeve's warriors couldn't
hide their pride as they gave the silver wheat and the
golden corn to the people. While they were away the
sun had come out again and their own corn was
beginning to ripen. The people who measured corn
said that if the corn now growing could all be taken
safely into the barns there would be just enough to do
till the next summer grew a new harvest. But just
when the corn in the fields was ripe the black pigs
came in from Ulster one night and began to eat it off
the stalks and leave only flattened straw wherever they
passed. People looking out through the holes in their
huts saw the corn falling and the gleaming eyes of the
dark pigs like little moving moons. The eyes moved
close to the huts but the pigs themselves could not be
seen on the dark nights of that September.

Queen Maeve called her council of war but none of
her warriors knew what to do till an old man with a
black beard rode into Maeve's palace on a white horse
and said that the pigs could only be beaten when the
skin of one of them was stretched between four hills

and the rain of a wet night allowed to fall into it. But he didn't know how the pig might be caught. Nor did any of Maeve's warriors and every night the bright eyes moved out of the forests and every morning the people awoke to the sight of more ploughed and trampled fields.

One night Maeve sent out her soldiers to kill them but the pigs leaped at them and knocked them from their horses and their horses took fright and galloped into the sea. She sent men to string ropes of scutch through the corn so that the pigs might become entangled in them. But the pigs pulled the ropes and wrapped them around trees to trip the horses of any warrior who came out in the night. Maeve then sent her best warriors to trap them in walls of fire but the pigs breathed on the flames and blew them all over the countryside, setting fire to huts and sending the people scurrying into the safety of the lakes.

Then, when Maeve was at her wits' end she herself and her very best warriors went out to do combat with them. The pigs came rushing at them, led by the blackest one, their fierce tusks brighter than their angry eyes. Seven warriors galloped towards them but the pigs leaped at them, knocked them from their horses and gored them with their fierce tusks before the other warriors could even move. Seven more warriors rode out and their horses were kicked to the pig. That lake is still there to-day in the middle of what is now County Monaghan.

And some people call it Much Shnamh or the pig's swim because before the night was out and all the pigs were dead, one of them, which was said to be the witch woman herself, swam across the lake and began to throw up the ground with her feet. All night she ran wildly in the rain, uprooting trees, shovelling the earth frantically and allowing the rain to settle in the trenches she had made. Towards morning the rain stopped and as the sky began to brighten over the lands of Ulster and Connacht the people could see the wheat broken and flattened to the ground as if a whole army had walked across it.

Queen Maeve rode to the top of the Ox mountains and she looked north towards the province of Ulster just as the sun was beginning to rise. The final screeches of the dying pigs were making the air tremble and near the Lough of Erin the earth itself seemed to be moving into the gaps between the hills, making a ditch as high as the hills themselves all around the province of Ulster. With the rising of the sun the last black pig went into its final torment and, its fortress-dyke completed, let out a howl which could be heard in the Isle of Man and buried itself in the ditch it had made.

During that winter the men of Ulster built battlements on top of the dyke while the men of Connacht starved in their wheatless barns, bemoaning the loss of loved ones and of the great warriors who had died. By the end of the year the battlements on top of the Black Pig's Dyke had been completed and Maeve knew that, for her, the straight route to Ulster had been closed forever. The corn grew the next year in both halves of the divided land.

John McArdle